DINOSAUR
Questions & Answers!

Published by the Natural History Museum, London

Q What are dinosaurs?

A Dinosaurs are a group of reptiles that are closely related to modern crocodiles and birds. They ruled life on Earth for over 160 million years. Then most of them suddenly disappeared in a dramatic extinction.

Crow

Bambiraptor
bam-bee-rap-tor

Small two-legged dinosaurs called theropods evolved into birds.

Q When did dinosaurs live?

A They lived between 245 and 66 million years ago, but they didn't all live at the same time.

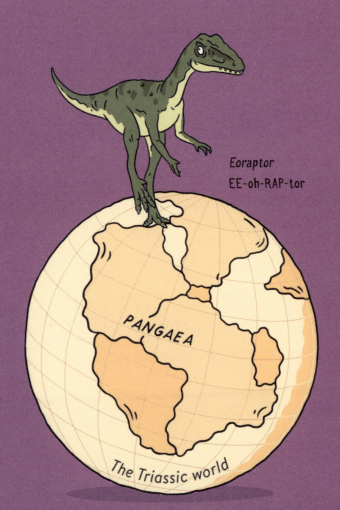

Eoraptor
EE-oh-RAP-tor

PANGAEA

The Triassic world

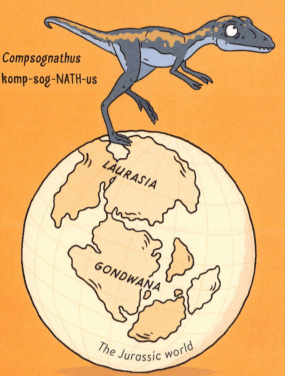

Compsognathus
komp-sog-NATH-us

The Jurassic world

Dinosaurs lived in a time known as the Mesozoic Era. Scientists divide this into three periods: the Triassic (252 to 201 million years ago), the Jurassic (201 to 145 million years ago) and the Cretaceous (145 to 66 million years ago).

During dinosaur times the land, that started as one big continent called Pangaea, slowly drifted apart into the seven continents that we know today.

Sauropelta
sore-oh-pelt-ah

The Cretaceous world

Q Where did dinosaurs live?

A All over the world. Dinosaur fossils have been found on every continent on Earth.

Cryolophosaurus
cry-o-loaf-oh-sore-us

Antarctica was once covered in lush, green forests and *Cryolophosaurus* lived there. It is one of only eight named dinosaurs that have been found in this now icy environment.

In Mongolia's Gobi Desert, dinosaur bones are often found just under the surface. Small dinosaurs like *Byronosaurus* and *Velociraptor* have been found there.

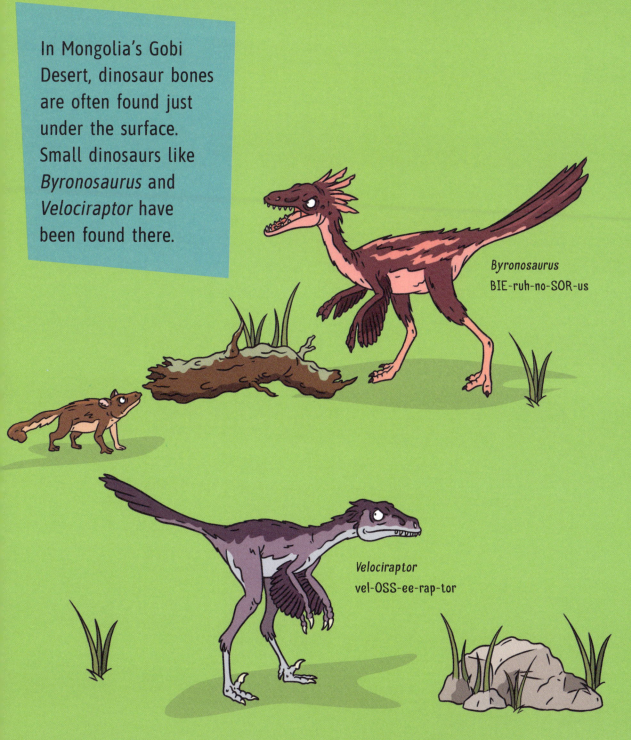

Byronosaurus
BIE-ruh-no-SOR-us

Velociraptor
vel-OSS-ee-rap-tor

Q What was the world like when dinosaurs were alive?

A In the Triassic it was hot and dry like a desert. In the Jurassic it was warm and wet with lots of green plants. In the Cretaceous there were trees, swamps and the first flowering plants. There were no people, buildings or roads.

Today the biggest land animals are mammals. During dinosaur times mammals were no bigger than a cat.

Early mammal

Plesiosaurus
plee-SEE-uh-saw-rus

Large, fierce reptiles that weren't dinosaurs swam in the seas.

Kronosaurus
kro-no-SAW-rus

Q How long did dinosaurs live for?

A Large long-necked dinosaurs like *Alamosaurus* could live for over 50 years. The larger the dinosaur, the longer it lived.

Plateosaurus
plat-ee-oh-sore-us

Plateosaurus lived for 20 to 25 years.

Q How do we know about dinosaurs?

A All the information we have about dinosaurs comes from fossils. And sometimes they are very incomplete.

Scientists can tell the age of a dinosaur by counting the growth rings in a slice of its fossilized bone, just like you can find out the age of a tree by counting its growth rings. But they have to use a special microscope.

Argentinosaurus
AR-gent-eeno-sore-us

By studying animals alive today, scientists can work out what the parts of some dinosaurs looked like. For example, they can work out what the giant long necked dinosaurs' feet were like by studying elephants' feet.

Q How many bones does a dinosaur have?

A Several hundred individual bones, but it's rare to find a complete skeleton.

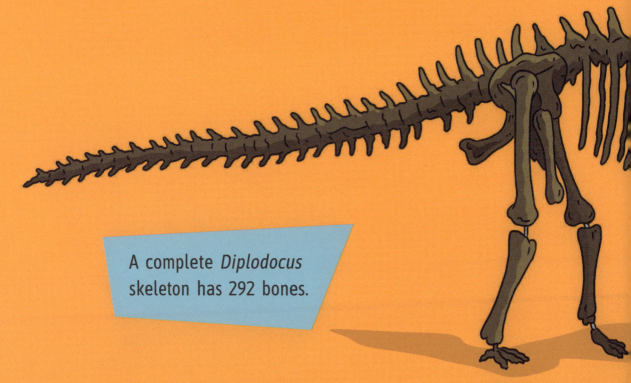

A complete *Diplodocus* skeleton has 292 bones.

The most complete *Tyrannosaurus rex* ever found has 250 bones – humans only have 206.

T. rex skull

Diplodocus
Dip-low-doh-cus

Q How many different dinosaurs were there?

A Hundreds. About 700 species of dinosaur have been discovered so far.

Megalosaurus
MEG-ah-low-sore-us

The first dinosaur fossil to be recognised as a dinosaur was in 1815 and belonged to *Megalosaurus*, a large predator that stalked coastal shores. Dinosaur fossils were discovered earlier, but they weren't recognised. They were thought to be the bones of giant humans!

Q Can we tell whether dinosaurs were male or female?

A It is very difficult as the skeletons of male and female dinosaurs are very similar. The only way to know if a dinosaur is a female is to find unlaid eggs inside her, and this has only happened twice in *Oviraptors*.

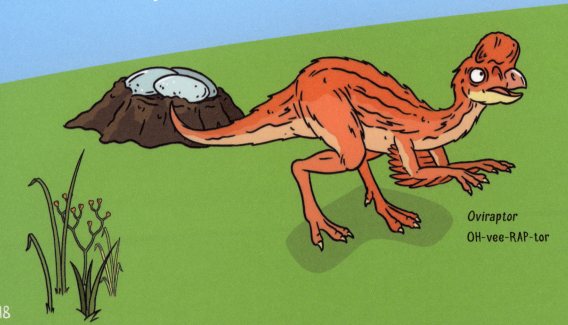

Oviraptor
OH-vee-RAP-tor

Dinosaur eggs came in various shapes and sizes and could reach up to 60 cm (23½ in) in length.

Egg comparison

Oviraptor egg

Ostrich egg

Chicken egg

Styracosaurus
sty-RAK-oh-sore-us

It's possible that the sizes and colours of the frills and horns of male and female dinosaurs were different.

19

Q Were dinosaurs good parents?

A Some were and they protected their eggs until they hatched, and then cared for their young. Some scientists think that some of the largest dinosaurs just laid their eggs and walked away.

The shell of the egg protected the baby dinosaur inside while it developed.

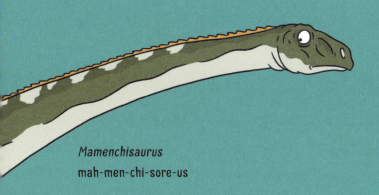

Mamenchisaurus
mah-men-chi-sore-us

Maiasaura
my-ah-SORE-ah

Maiasaura laid its eggs in a huge nest that it built on the ground.

21

Q What did dinosaurs eat?

A Some dinosaurs ate meat and we call them carnivores. Others chomped on plants and are known as herbivores. A few had a diet of meat and plants and are called omnivores.

Allosaurus
AL-oh-saw-russ

Some dinosaurs weren't very good at chewing tough food, like twigs and pine needles, so they swallowed small stones. The stones are called gastroliths and they helped grind up the plants they ate.

Kotasaurus
KOH-tuh-SORE-us

Allosaurus used its head like an axe. It used its strong neck muscles to ram its jaw into the body of its prey, then tore the flesh by pulling its head back and upward.

Q Were there more carnivores or herbivores?

A There were a lot more herbivores. More plant-eating dinosaurs have been identified than meat-eating ones, but there may be more waiting to be discovered. On average, one dinosaur is named a week.

Apatosaurus
ah-PAT-oh-sore-us

Large meat-eating dinosaurs could eat one big meal and then eat nothing else for weeks.

Becklespinax
Beck-el-spine-axe

Herbivores grazed all day, eating huge amounts of vegetation. Some didn't even need to chew their food, they just swallowed it whole and their guts fermented it.

25

Q What happened if a dinosaur broke a tooth?

A It would grow another one, just like sharks do today. In fact, dinosaurs, like all reptiles, continually replaced their teeth throughout their lives. It's only mammals that don't do this.

Thecodontosaurus
theek-o-don-toh-sore-us

Dilophosaurus was a quick and fearsome meat-eating dinosaur. A kink in its upper jaw meant that it was able to grip and hold onto its prey, like crocodiles do today.

Dilophosaurus
die-LOAF-oh-sore-us

Thecodontosaurus had serrated, leaf-shaped teeth that suggest it was a herbivore.

Q Which dinosaur had the biggest teeth?

A The biggest and most fearsome teeth were about 30 cm or 12 in long and belonged to T. rex.

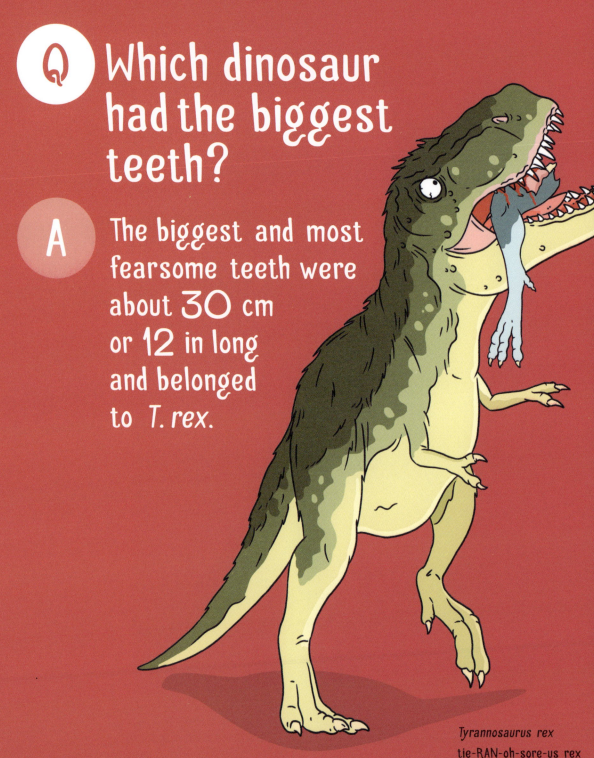

Tyrannosaurus rex
tie-RAN-oh-sore-us rex

Herrerasaurus had an unusual hinged bottom jaw, which helped it to grip its struggling prey very tightly.

Herrerasaurus
herr-ray-rah-SORE-us

T. rex's pointed, serrated teeth sliced through chunks of meat and crunched bones easily. Its bite was three times more powerful than a lion's bite.

Q Did dinosaurs poop?

A Yes, but when their poo is found it isn't soft and smelly, it is fossilized and looks like hard mud or stone.

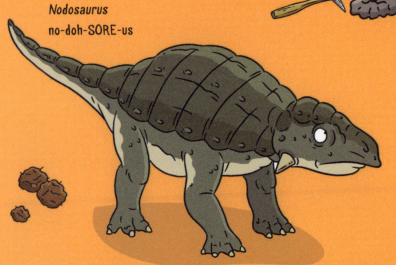

Nodosaurus
no-doh-SORE-us

Fossilized poo is called coprolite.

Q What colours were dinosaurs?

A Nobody really knows but scientists can work out certain colours from impressions in rocks of dinosaur feathers and skin. Probably some were brightly coloured and others were dull.

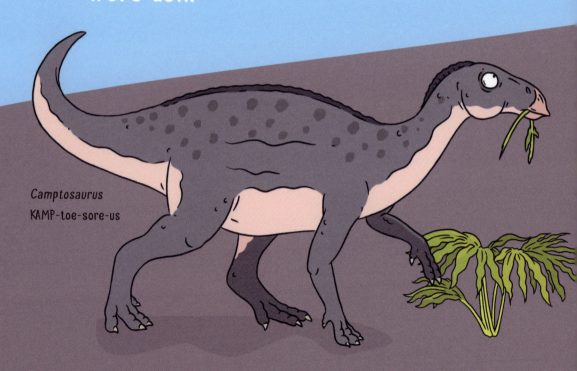

Camptosaurus
KAMP-toe-sore-us

Just like some lizards today, *Liliensternus* may have flashed its coloured head crest to scare away rivals.

Liliensternus
lil-ee-en-stern-us

In some fossils, skin cells have been preserved that can tell us about colour. Each colour has a different shaped skin cell. From the shape of the cell scientists can tell what colour the dinosaur was.

Q What was dinosaur skin like?

A Fossils show evidence of different skin types — bumps, scales and armour. Not much dinosaur skin has survived so it is hard to know for sure.

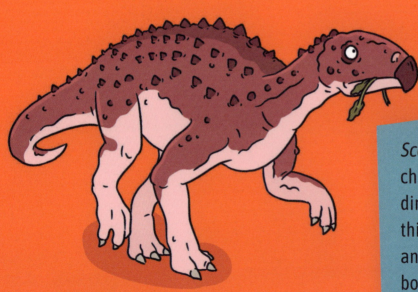

Scelidosaurus
skel-EYE-doh-sore-us

Scelidosaurus was a chunky four-footed dinosaur that had a thick armour of lumps and bumps made of bone. Amazingly these were covered with keratin, which is found in your fingernails.

Some plant-eating dinosaurs like *Euoplocephalus* had thick bony plates over their upper bodies, including their eyelids. These bony plates protected them against sharp-toothed attackers.

Q Did dinosaurs have feathers?

A Yes, some did. Fossilized impressions of feathers have been found in rock next to the bones of many meat-eating dinosaurs.

Yutyrannus
yoo-tie-RAN-us

Yutyrannus is the largest feathered dinosaur to be found so far. It was a fearsome hunter, very similar to *T. rex*, and probably used its feathers to keep warm.

Microraptor
MIKE-row-rap-tor

Caudipteryx
core-dip-ter-ix

Male birds are known to use their coloured feathers to impress females with dazzling displays. Perhaps some dinosaurs did the same.

Chirostenotes
kie-ro-sten-oh-teez

Some pterosaurs had wings as wide as an aeroplane.

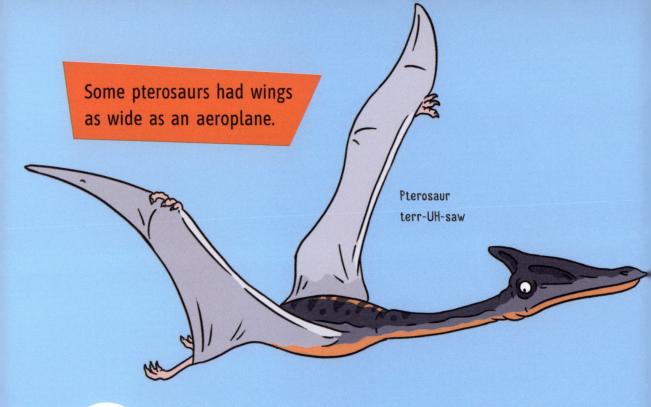

Pterosaur
terr-UH-saw

Q Could dinosaurs fly?

A Yes, some small feathered dinosaurs could fly but only for very short distances. And when the dinosaurs lived there were flying reptiles, but these were not dinosaurs and they belonged to a different group of animals called pterosaurs.

Dino-bird *Archaeopteryx* could flap its long feathery arms to fly short distances.

Archaeopteryx
ark-ee-OPT-er-ix

Q Could dinosaurs swim?

A We're not sure. Fossilized tracks on riverbeds show that at least some of them entered water, even if it was just to hunt.

Spinosaurus
SPINE-oh-SORE-us

Scientists once thought that *Parasaurolophus* lived in water, using its crest, which grew from its nose bones, as a snorkel. It is more likely to have used its crest to honk like a trumpet.

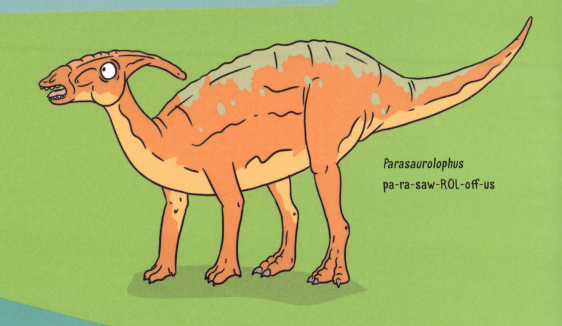

Parasaurolophus
pa-ra-saw-ROL-off-us

Spinosaurus was among the largest land meat-eating dinosaurs. And it is one of the only dinosaurs known to eat a regular diet of fish.

Argentinosaurus
AR-gent-eeno-sore-us

Q **Which dinosaur was the biggest?**

A It's hard to say because complete skeletons of dinosaurs are rarely found. The massive herbivorous sauropods were definitely some of the biggest!

Argentinosaurus could weigh as much as 12 African elephants and was as long as three London buses.

Sauroposeidon
SORE-o-po-SY-don

Sauroposeidon is the tallest sauropod ever known. It was 18 m or 59 ft tall, which is about as high as a four or five storey building.

Q Which dinosaur was the fastest?

A It's very difficult to work out but some scientists think one of the fastest was *Struthiomimus*. It could run up to 60 km/h or 37 mph, similar to an ostrich today.

The slowest dinosaurs were sauropods. Their top speed was similar to a human's walking pace, about 8 km/h or 5 mph.

Q Why did some dinosaurs have such short arms?

A Because they didn't need them to catch food. They could easily grab smaller dinosaurs with their powerful jaws, but they might have used their arms to hold down their prey while they chomped on them.

Giganotosaurus
gig-an-OH-toe-SORE-us

Tiny arms may look useless, but fossils show that they were quite strong and muscly. They could have been used to slash at prey or other dinosaurs in fights.

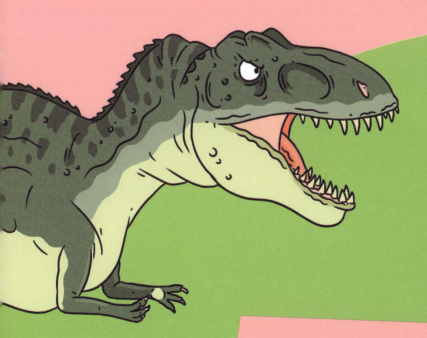

Over time, as these dinosaurs evolved, their arms became shorter and eventually they were no longer needed. They were on their way to losing them.

Q Which dinosaur had the biggest claws?

A The plant-eating dinosaur *Nothronychus* had the longest claws of any animal, reaching up to 1 m or 3 ft long.

Baryonyx
bah-ree-ON-icks

Baryonyx had one huge 30 cm or 12 in claw on each hand, which it might have used to hook fish out of the water to eat.

Q What sounds did dinosaurs make?

A No-one really knows because the soft structure in the neck that a dinosaur needs to make sounds doesn't fossilize so has never been found.

Torvosaurus
TOR-voh-SORE-us

The hollow head crest of *Lambeosaurus* was probably used as a chamber for making deep bellowing sounds, similar to a horn.

Lambeosaurus
lam-BEE-oh-SORE-us

Dinosaurs might have made all sorts of noises, just like living birds and crocodiles make today.

Q How smart were dinosaurs?

A It's hard to say. Experts think some of the meat-eating dinosaurs were as smart as today's birds.

Troodon
TROH-oh-don

Troodon had one of the biggest brains for its body size and was probably one of the smartest. It was also one of the smallest dinosaurs.

Stegosaurus is famous for having a tiny brain. Its body was as big as a large van, but its brain was the size of a plum.

Stegosaurus
STEG-oh-SORE-us

Q Why did some dinosaurs have bony heads?

A Probably to compete with each other or to defend themselves against attackers.

Pachycephalosaurus
pack-ee-kef-ah-lo-sore-us

Pachycephalosaurus was the largest bone-headed dinosaur. Its skull was 25 cm or 10 in thick. Males may have banged their bony heads together to fight over females.

Pachyrhinosaurus had a large, bulky, rough area of flat bone covering the top of its nose. It might have used this to ram other dinosaurs that got in its way.

Pachyrhinosaurus
pack-ee-RINE-oh-sore-us

Q What did dinosaurs use their tails for?

A Dinosaurs with long necks and heavy heads used their long tails for balance, otherwise they might topple over.

Ankylosaurus
an-KIE-loh-sore-us

Shunosaurus
SHOON-oh-SORE-us

Some dinosaurs with long tails used them as whips, that they may have swung at their attackers to keep them away.

Club-tailed dinosaurs used the hard, bony clubs at the ends of their tails to strike out at other dinosaurs, maybe breaking their bones.

T. rex's arms couldn't reach its mouth!

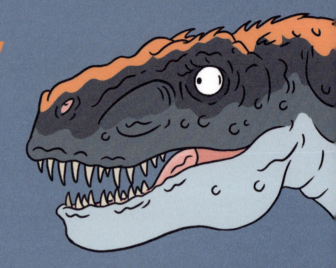

Q **If *T. rex* fell over how would it get back up?**

A It probably did what birds do when they fall over – get up in a very undignified way, wiggle around, kick its legs and feet and use its head to lever itself up off the ground.

Tyrannosaurus rex
tie-RAN-oh-sore-us rex

T. rex had an excellent sense of smell. It could easily sniff out and locate dead bodies to scavenge.

Q What killed the dinosaurs?

A A massive rock from space, called a meteor, smashed into the Earth. It created so much dust that it blocked out the Sun for many years.

Early mammal

Many animals died after the meteor struck, but not all. Lots of small animals survived by sheltering from the dust and finding enough to eat.

Triceratops
try-SERRA-tops

Most of the dead animals were eaten or simply rotted away, but some remains were preserved under the ground, and in time turned into fossils.

Q **Why are birds the only surviving dinosaurs?**

A The dinosaurs that survived the mass extinction were no bigger than chickens. Small creatures produce offspring faster, don't need to eat much and adapt more quickly to new surroundings. This all helped the dinosaurs that were birds survive.

Presbyornis
prez-bee-OR-nis

Confuciusornis was an early crow-sized dinosaur. It spent most of its time at the tops of trees to avoid being eaten by other dinosaurs, and used its wings to glide through the air.

Confuciusornis
kon-few-shus-or-niss

Goose-like *Presbyornis* evolved soon after dinosaurs became extinct. It used its broad, flat bill to filter food from the water, like geese and ducks do today.

First published by the Natural History Museum, Cromwell Road, London SW7 5BD

© The Trustees of the Natural History Museum, London, 2021

All rights reserved. No part of this publication may be transmitted in any form or by any means without prior permission from the British publisher.

A catalogue record for this book is available from the British Library.

ISBN 978 0 56509 515 4

10 9 8 7 6 5 4 3 2 1

Internal design by Bobby Birchall, Bobby&Co
Reproduction by Saxon Digital Services
Printed in China by Toppan Leefung Ltd

All illustrations © Andy Forshaw, What on Earth Publishing.

Special thanks to Dr Susannah Maidment and Dr Paul Barrett at the Natural History Museum for checking the text and illustrations.

Carnotaurus
Kar-noh-TORE-us